THE WRITER'S COMPLETE SERIES BIBLE WORKBOOK

CELIA KYLE

Printed in the United States of America

First Printing, 2018

ISBN 978-1-68039-002-5

Novel Notes
2885 Sanford Ave SW #26314
Grandville, MI 49418
www.novelnotesbooks.com

Ordering Information:

Quantity sales. Special discounts are available on quantity purchases by corporations, associations, and others. For details, contact the publisher at the address above.

Orders by U.S. trade bookstores and wholesalers. Please contact Ingram Content Group: Tel: (615) 793-5000 or visit www.ingramcontent.com.

Praise

"As a working author with multiple series going at any given time, anything that helps track book information is invaluable. *The Writer's Complete Series Bible Workbook's* layout is simple, easy to use, and customizable for all fiction genres. Printing the worksheets makes personalizing a series bible binder fast and easy and creates extra pages that are useful when brainstorming a new idea or plot thread."

- Michelle M. Pillow
NYT & USAT Bestselling Author of the *Dragon Lords* and *Warlocks MacGregor* series

"Where has this been all my life? No, seriously?"

- Ruby Dixon

Table of Contents

Acknowledgements — 7

Introduction — 9

Series Information — 11

World Rules, Series Notes & Definitions of Terms — 13

Quick Reference Lists — 27

Main Character Details — 33

Secondary Character Details — 77

Settings — 89

Book Summaries — 109

Notes — 141

Acknowledgments

I'd like to send out great big, squishy hugs to everyone who made this workbook possible. From Marina Maddix (who apparently got a geek girl boner after a glimpse at the first draft) to all of the wonderful authors who peeked at an early version of the workbook and gave me awesome feedback. Here's a list of the luverly authors who put in their two cents (sometimes a lot more) so that I could wrap this project and hit the publish button.

In no particular order…

Marina Maddix

Abbie Zanders

Bianca D'Arc

Reina Torres

Tonya Brooks

Michelle M. Pillow

Gwen Knight

Ruby Dixon

Cynthia Sax

Theodora Taylor

Kasey Bell

Hailey Edwards

Everleigh Clark

> One of the biggest lies I tell myself is *"I don't need to write that down, I'll remember it."*
>
> ~Everyone Ever

Introduction

Welcome to *The Writer's Complete Series Bible Workbook!* The original title was: *Celia Needed a Series Bible and Making it Available to Others Sounded Like a Good Idea.* Since that was difficult to fit on a book cover, and no one knew who the heck this "Celia" person was, the title was changed.

But just because the title changed doesn't mean the content was altered in any way. From beginning to end, this is exactly what I use when creating and tracking everything that happens in one of my series. It helps keep me organized while also making sure that all of those nitpicky (and not not-so-nitpicky) facts remain at my fingertips.

Now, some writers might look at this workbook and scoff. "I don't need a series bible! I remember everything about everything!" Um, sure. As my fellow southerners say, "Bless your heart."

Let me tell you a story. Once upon a time, a certain author (*cough* me *cough*) wrote a dragon shapeshifting alien romance. It sold amazingly well, readers loved it, and I had an awesome time writing the book. So, of course, I decided to make it a series and write book two! *high five*

Did I go back and make notes about what happened in book one? No.

Did I go back and re-read book one before I started book two? No.

Did I screw up in book two so badly that readers emailed me on release day, telling me that I screwed up? YES.

You see, the hero in book two had an injury that shaped him as an individual and played an integral part in the story. He was a dragon shapeshifting alien *without wings*. Sure, he'd lost them in this amazing battle, but not having wings was a *huge* deal in that world of alien dragons. You weren't a dragon if you didn't have *wings*.

Ask me what I did. Go ahead. Ask. Because, yes, I wrote several scenes where the wingless hero *did things with wings.* Things that could *only* be done if he had wings. He shielded the heroine *with his wings*. He cuddled the heroine close *with his wings*. He *flew.*

Sure, I hurried and made the corrections before re-uploading the file, but the damage was done. I'd disappointed those early readers. The one thing I could have done to avoid the problem was to take some time to re-read book one and write things down. And thus, the early versions of *The Writer's Complete Series Bible Workbook* was born in a composition notebook.

Series Information

Series Name ______________________________

Genre ______________________________

Book Title ______________________ Book # __________

eBook ISBN ______________ Amazon ASIN ______________

Print ISBN ______________ Pub Date __________ Length __________

Book Title ______________________ Book # __________

eBook ISBN ______________ Amazon ASIN ______________

Print ISBN ______________ Pub Date __________ Length __________

Book Title ______________________ Book # __________

eBook ISBN ______________ Amazon ASIN ______________

Print ISBN ______________ Pub Date __________ Length __________

Book Title ______________________ Book # __________

eBook ISBN ______________ Amazon ASIN ______________

Print ISBN ______________ Pub Date __________ Length __________

Book Title ______________________ Book # __________

eBook ISBN ______________ Amazon ASIN ______________

Print ISBN ______________ Pub Date __________ Length __________

World Rules, Series Notes & Definitions of Terms

Here's where you'll write down the intricacies of your world and those nitpicky details that you're sure you'll remember later… and then you don't. Let's take a minute to go through exactly what you'll put in this section.

First up are your "World Rules." Those are hard and fast rules that can never ever be broken. For example, if you're writing about werewolves that can *only* shift at the full moon, you'd write that "World Rule" in this section.

"Series Notes" is a somewhat catch-all phrase used to describe bits of information you want to write down that don't necessarily have a home elsewhere within the workbook. One example of a "Series Note" would be that your werewolves (who can *only* shift at the full moon) originally appeared in the world in 1502. That fact doesn't have a place anywhere else within these pages, but it's definitely something that needs to be remembered.

Now we've come to "Definitions of Terms." I use this area for any words that I've made up, as well as any foreign-language words I use within the series. It can also be used to define made-up roles and jobs within your book. Our werewolves (who can only shift at the full moon and first appeared in the world in 1502) are led by a *Luna*. That's a word I decided to use as a title for the female werewolf who leads a werewolf pack.

Now that you know what belongs in this section… get to writing!

World Rules

Werewolves can only shift during the full moon.

Series Notes

Werewolves were first revealed in 1502.

Definitions of Terms

Luna - Female werewolf who rules a pack.

World Rules

World Rules

World Rules

World Rules

Series Notes

Series Notes

Series Notes

Series Notes

Definitions of Terms

Definitions of Terms

Definitions of Terms

Definitions of Terms

Quick Reference Lists

Sometimes when you're writing, you don't want to flip through every page of the workbook to find that *one* name or location you can't recall. That's where your handy-dandy "Quick Reference Lists" comes in!

Let's go through the three columns in the "Quick Reference Lists" quickly before I release you into the quick referencing world. Your first column is the "Character Name" or "Setting Name" column and you should include both your character's first and last name or the full name of your setting. For characters, I also find it helpful to include their nickname as well.

I use the "Brief Description" column for any small details that are particular to that character or setting. If we think back to our werewolves… (who are led by a Luna, can only shift during a full moon, and whose kind were originally found in 1502) I would add the character's position in the werewolf pack. (I.e. Luna) If the character is a human in my werewolf world and works as a plumber for the pack, I might write "human; pack plumber" in the "Brief Description" column. With this column filled, it'll be easy for me to find the name of the pack's plumber!

The last column references the page number of that character's detail page, where you'll find more —you guessed it— details about that character. Sure, you might know that Alex Davis is the pack's human plumber, but what if you want to know the color of his eyes? Well, flip on over to the detail page.

Character Quick Reference

Character Name	Brief Description	Workbook Page #
Caroline Wolfieton	Luna	

Setting Quick Refernce

Setting Name	Brief Description	Workbook Page #
Wolfieton Pack house	Mansion in the woods.	

Main Character Quick Reference

Character Name	Brief Description	Workbook Page #

Secondary Character Quick Reference

Character Name	Brief Description	Workbook Page #

Setting Quick Reference

Setting Name	Brief Description	Workbook Page #

Setting Quick Reference

Setting Name	Brief Description	Workbook Page #

Main Character Details

Now we're getting into the details of our characters. Our world is sketched out and we know who our characters are at a glance, but what makes them *them.* Here you'll keep track of your main characters' vital statistics, as well as their personality traits, relationship status, and any family connections they have to other characters in your world. You've also got a blank page to write down anything else that is important to your character. That could be anything from the fact our werewolf Luna is half-vampire to the fact that her favorite color is orange. Anything else that you deem important can go on that page.

When writing a novel a writer should create living people; people note characters. A character is a caricature.

~Ernest Hemingway

Name Caroline Wolfieton Nickname Caro

Age 34 Birthday August 21 Death Date Still Kicking!

Gender Female Species Werewolf

Residence Wolfieton Pack house

Job/Career Luna of the Wolfieton pack

Physical Description

Eye Color Blue Hair Color Blonde

Skin Color Light tan Height 5'10"

Build Curvy

Wolf is dark gray with white tips on ears/tail. Bigger than normal female wolves.

Personality Traits She kicks butt and doesn't hesitate to take down hot heads a few pegs or two.

Important Life Events Her father died when she was 18. Killed by rogue werewolves.

In a relationship with Eric Hotterton Workbook Pg # 123

Connections

Name	Relationship	Workbook Page #
George Wolfieton	Dec. Dad	155
Jeannie Wolfieton	Mom	156
Rebecca Liongreen	BFF	172

Main Character in Book #/Title #1

Other books this character appears in #2, #4, #5

Additional Notes

Dated her BFF's older brother for a hot minute but they're just friends now.

Name ____________ Nickname ____________

Age ______ Birthday ____________ Death Date ____________

Gender ____________ Species ____________

Residence ____________

Job/Career ____________

Physical Description

Eye Color ____________ Hair Color ____________

Skin Color ____________ Height ____________

Build ____________ ____________

Personality Traits ____________

Important Life Events ____________

In a relationship with ____________ Workbook Pg # ______

Connections

Name	Relationship	Workbook Page #

Main Character in Book #/Title ____________

Other books this character appears in ____________

Additional Notes

Name ____________________ Nickname ____________________

Age ________ Birthday ____________________ Death Date ____________________

Gender ____________________ Species ____________________

Residence ____

Job/Career ____

Physical Description

Eye Color ____________________ Hair Color ____________________

Skin Color ____________________ Height ____________________

Build ____________________ ____________________

Personality Traits ____

Important Life Events ____

In a relationship with ____________________ Workbook Pg # __________

Connections

Name	Relationship	Workbook Page #

Main Character in Book #/Title ____________________

Other books this character appears in ____________________

Additional Notes

Name ______________________ Nickname ______________________

Age __________ Birthday ______________________ Death Date ______________________

Gender ______________________ Species ______________________

Residence ______________________

Job/Career ______________________

Physical Description

Eye Color ______________________ Hair Color ______________________

Skin Color ______________________ Height ______________________

Build ______________________ ______________________

Personality Traits ______________________

Important Life Events ______________________

In a relationship with ______________________ Workbook Pg # __________

Connections

Name	Relationship	Workbook Page #

Main Character in Book #/Title ______________________

Other books this character appears in ______________________

Additional Notes

Name ______________________ Nickname ______________________

Age ________ Birthday ________________ Death Date ____________

Gender ______________________ Species ______________________

Residence ____

Job/Career ____

Physical Description

Eye Color ______________________ Hair Color ______________________

Skin Color ______________________ Height ______________________

Build ______________________ ______________________

Personality Traits ____

Important Life Events ____

In a relationship with ______________________ Workbook Pg # ________

Connections

Name	Relationship	Workbook Page #

Main Character in Book #/Title ______________________

Other books this character appears in ______________________

Additional Notes

Name ____________________ Nickname ____________________

Age ________ Birthday ____________________ Death Date ____________

Gender ____________________ Species ____________________

Residence ____

Job/Career ____

Physical Description

Eye Color ____________________ Hair Color ____________________

Skin Color ____________________ Height ____________________

Build ____________________ ____________________

____

____

Personality Traits ____

____

Important Life Events ____

____

In a relationship with ____________________ Workbook Pg # ________

Connections

Name	Relationship	Workbook Page #

Main Character in Book #/Title ____________________

Other books this character appears in ____________________

Additional Notes

Name ______________________ Nickname ______________________

Age __________ Birthday ______________________ Death Date ______________

Gender ______________________ Species ______________________

Residence ____

Job/Career ____

Physical Description

Eye Color ______________________ Hair Color ______________________

Skin Color ______________________ Height ______________________

Build ______________________ ______________________

Personality Traits ____

Important Life Events ____

In a relationship with ______________________ Workbook Pg # __________

Connections

Name	Relationship	Workbook Page #

Main Character in Book #/Title ______________________

Other books this character appears in ______________________

Additional Notes

Name ______________________ Nickname ______________________

Age __________ Birthday ______________________ Death Date ______________

Gender ______________________ Species ______________________

Residence ____

Job/Career ____

Physical Description

Eye Color ______________________ Hair Color ______________________

Skin Color ______________________ Height ______________________

Build ______________________ ______________________

____

____

Personality Traits ____

____

Important Life Events ____

____

In a relationship with ______________________ Workbook Pg # __________

Connections

Name	Relationship	Workbook Page #

Main Character in Book #/Title ______________________

Other books this character appears in ______________________

Additional Notes

Name ______________________ Nickname ______________________

Age __________ Birthday ______________________ Death Date ______________

Gender ______________________ Species ______________________

Residence ____

Job/Career ____

Physical Description

Eye Color ______________________ Hair Color ______________________

Skin Color ______________________ Height ______________________

Build ______________________ ______________________

____

____

Personality Traits ____

____

Important Life Events ____

____

In a relationship with ______________________ Workbook Pg # __________

Connections

Name	Relationship	Workbook Page #

Main Character in Book #/Title ______________________

Other books this character appears in ______________________

Additional Notes

Name ______________________ Nickname ______________________

Age __________ Birthday ______________________ Death Date ______________

Gender ______________________ Species ______________________

Residence ____

Job/Career ____

Physical Description

Eye Color ______________________ Hair Color ______________________

Skin Color ______________________ Height ______________________

Build ______________________ ______________________

____

____

Personality Traits ____

____

Important Life Events ____

____

In a relationship with ______________________ Workbook Pg # __________

Connections

Name	Relationship	Workbook Page #

Main Character in Book #/Title ____

Other books this character appears in ____

Additional Notes

Name ____________ Nickname ____________

Age ______ Birthday ____________ Death Date ____________

Gender ____________ Species ____________

Residence ____________

Job/Career ____________

Physical Description

Eye Color ____________ Hair Color ____________

Skin Color ____________ Height ____________

Build ____________ ____________

____

____

Personality Traits ____________

____

Important Life Events ____________

____

In a relationship with ____________ Workbook Pg # ______

Connections

Name	Relationship	Workbook Page #

Main Character in Book #/Title ____________

Other books this character appears in ____________

Additional Notes

Name ______________________ Nickname ______________________

Age __________ Birthday ______________________ Death Date ______________

Gender ______________________ Species ______________________

Residence ____

Job/Career ____

Physical Description

Eye Color ______________________ Hair Color ______________________

Skin Color ______________________ Height ______________________

Build ______________________ ______________________

Personality Traits ____

Important Life Events ____

In a relationship with ______________________ Workbook Pg # __________

Connections

Name	Relationship	Workbook Page #

Main Character in Book #/Title ____

Other books this character appears in ____

Additional Notes

Name ______________________ Nickname ______________________

Age ________ Birthday ________________ Death Date ______________

Gender ______________________ Species ______________________

Residence ____

Job/Career ____

Physical Description

Eye Color ______________________ Hair Color ______________________

Skin Color ______________________ Height ______________________

Build ______________________ ______________________

____

____

Personality Traits ____

____

Important Life Events ____

____

In a relationship with ______________________ Workbook Pg # __________

Connections

Name	Relationship	Workbook Page #

Main Character in Book #/Title ____

Other books this character appears in ____

Additional Notes

Name ______________________ Nickname ______________________

Age __________ Birthday ______________________ Death Date ______________

Gender ______________________ Species ______________________

Residence ____

Job/Career ____

Physical Description

Eye Color ______________________ Hair Color ______________________

Skin Color ______________________ Height ______________________

Build ______________________ ______________________

____

____

Personality Traits ____

____

Important Life Events ____

____

In a relationship with ______________________ Workbook Pg # __________

Connections

Name	Relationship	Workbook Page #

Main Character in Book #/Title ______________________

Other books this character appears in ______________________

Additional Notes

Name ______________________ Nickname ______________________

Age ________ Birthday ________________ Death Date ______________

Gender ______________________ Species ______________________

Residence ____

Job/Career ____

Physical Description

Eye Color ______________________ Hair Color ______________________

Skin Color ______________________ Height ______________________

Build ______________________ ______________________

____

____

Personality Traits ____

____

Important Life Events ____

____

In a relationship with ______________________ Workbook Pg # ________

Connections

Name	Relationship	Workbook Page #

Main Character in Book #/Title ____

Other books this character appears in ____

Additional Notes

Name ______________________ Nickname ______________________

Age __________ Birthday ______________________ Death Date ______________

Gender ______________________ Species ______________________

Residence ____

Job/Career ____

Physical Description

Eye Color ______________________ Hair Color ______________________

Skin Color ______________________ Height ______________________

Build ______________________ ______________________

____

____

Personality Traits ____

____

Important Life Events ____

____

In a relationship with ______________________ Workbook Pg # __________

Connections

Name	Relationship	Workbook Page #

Main Character in Book #/Title ____

Other books this character appears in ____

Additional Notes

Name ______________________ Nickname ______________________

Age __________ Birthday ______________________ Death Date ______________

Gender ______________________ Species ______________________

Residence ____

Job/Career ____

Physical Description

Eye Color ______________________ Hair Color ______________________

Skin Color ______________________ Height ______________________

Build ______________________ ______________________

____

____

Personality Traits ____

____

Important Life Events ____

____

In a relationship with ______________________ Workbook Pg # __________

Connections

Name	Relationship	Workbook Page #

Main Character in Book #/Title ______________________

Other books this character appears in ______________________

Additional Notes

Name ______________________ Nickname ______________________

Age __________ Birthday ______________________ Death Date ______________

Gender ______________________ Species ______________________

Residence ____

Job/Career ____

Physical Description

Eye Color ______________________ Hair Color ______________________

Skin Color ______________________ Height ______________________

Build ______________________ ______________________

Personality Traits ____

Important Life Events ____

In a relationship with ______________________ Workbook Pg # __________

Connections

Name	Relationship	Workbook Page #

Main Character in Book #/Title ____

Other books this character appears in ____

Additional Notes

Name ______________________ Nickname ______________________

Age __________ Birthday ______________________ Death Date ______________

Gender ______________________ Species ______________________

Residence ____

Job/Career ____

Physical Description

Eye Color ______________________ Hair Color ______________________

Skin Color ______________________ Height ______________________

Build ______________________ ______________________

____

____

Personality Traits ____

____

Important Life Events ____

____

In a relationship with ______________________ Workbook Pg # __________

Connections

Name	Relationship	Workbook Page #

Main Character in Book #/Title ______________________

Other books this character appears in ______________________

Additional Notes

Name ______________________ Nickname ______________________

Age __________ Birthday ______________________ Death Date ______________

Gender ______________________ Species ______________________

Residence ____

Job/Career ____

Physical Description

Eye Color ______________________ Hair Color ______________________

Skin Color ______________________ Height ______________________

Build ______________________ ______________________

____

____

Personality Traits ____

____

Important Life Events ____

____

In a relationship with ______________________ Workbook Pg # __________

Connections

Name	Relationship	Workbook Page #

Main Character in Book #/Title ____

Other books this character appears in ____

Additional Notes

Name ______________________ Nickname ______________________

Age __________ Birthday ______________________ Death Date ______________

Gender ______________________ Species ______________________

Residence ____

Job/Career ____

Physical Description

Eye Color ______________________ Hair Color ______________________

Skin Color ______________________ Height ______________________

Build ______________________ ______________________

____

____

Personality Traits ____

____

Important Life Events ____

____

In a relationship with ______________________ Workbook Pg # __________

Connections

Name	Relationship	Workbook Page #

Main Character in Book #/Title ____

Other books this character appears in ____

Additional Notes

Additional Notes

Secondary Character Details

Remember our human werewolf pack plumber? Well, if he's not one of your book's leading men, you'll make notes about him in this section. These characters might not be worthy of their own book but are still important to your story. What if our werewolf pack plumber is the Luna's ex-boy toy? If a secondary character impacts your story, but isn't going to receive their own story, you'd write down their information in this section.

Name Jeannie Wolfieton
Nickname N/A
Age 68
Birthday June 16
Death Date Not yet!
Gender Female
Species Werewolf
Physical Appearance
Eye Color Blue
Hair Color Blonde
Skin Color Tanned
Height 5'11"
Build Curvy

Role Caroline's mom
Job/Career Teaches werewolf pups
Books this character appears in #1
Other Notes She isn't afraid to throw a frying pan at someone if they get out of line.

Name ______________________ Nickname ______________

Age ________ Birthday ______________ Death Date ______________

Gender ______________ Species ______________

Physical Appearance

Eye Color ______________ Hair Color ______________

Skin Color ______________ Height ______________

Build ______________

Role ______________ Job/Career ______________

Books this character appears in ______________

Other Notes ______________

Name ______________________ Nickname ______________

Age ________ Birthday ______________ Death Date ______________

Gender ______________ Species ______________

Physical Appearance

Eye Color ______________ Hair Color ______________

Skin Color ______________ Height ______________

Build ______________

Role ______________ Job/Career ______________

Books this character appears in ______________

Other Notes ______________

Name ____________________ Nickname ____________
Age ______ Birthday ______________ Death Date ____________
Gender ____________ Species ____________
Physical Appearance
Eye Color ____________ Hair Color ____________
Skin Color ____________ Height ____________
Build ____________ ____________

Role ____________ Job/Career ____________
Books this character appears in ____________
Other Notes ____________

Name ____________________ Nickname ____________
Age ______ Birthday ______________ Death Date ____________
Gender ____________ Species ____________
Physical Appearance
Eye Color ____________ Hair Color ____________
Skin Color ____________ Height ____________
Build ____________ ____________

Role ____________ Job/Career ____________
Books this character appears in ____________
Other Notes ____________

Name ______ Nickname ______

Age ______ Birthday ______ Death Date ______

Gender ______ Species ______

Physical Appearance

Eye Color ______ Hair Color ______

Skin Color ______ Height ______

Build ______

Role ______ Job/Career ______

Books this character appears in ______

Other Notes ______

Name ______ Nickname ______

Age ______ Birthday ______ Death Date ______

Gender ______ Species ______

Physical Appearance

Eye Color ______ Hair Color ______

Skin Color ______ Height ______

Build ______

Role ______ Job/Career ______

Books this character appears in ______

Other Notes ______

Name ______________________ Nickname ______________

Age ________ Birthday ______________ Death Date ______________

Gender ______________ Species ______________

Physical Appearance

Eye Color ______________ Hair Color ______________

Skin Color ______________ Height ______________

Build ______________ ______________

____

Role ______________ Job/Career ______________

Books this character appears in ______________

Other Notes ______________________________

____

____

Name ______________________ Nickname ______________

Age ________ Birthday ______________ Death Date ______________

Gender ______________ Species ______________

Physical Appearance

Eye Color ______________ Hair Color ______________

Skin Color ______________ Height ______________

Build ______________ ______________

____

Role ______________ Job/Career ______________

Books this character appears in ______________

Other Notes ______________________________

____

____

Name ______ Nickname ______

Age ______ Birthday ______ Death Date ______

Gender ______ Species ______

Physical Appearance

Eye Color ______ Hair Color ______

Skin Color ______ Height ______

Build ______

Role ______ Job/Career ______

Books this character appears in ______

Other Notes ______

Name ______ Nickname ______

Age ______ Birthday ______ Death Date ______

Gender ______ Species ______

Physical Appearance

Eye Color ______ Hair Color ______

Skin Color ______ Height ______

Build ______

Role ______ Job/Career ______

Books this character appears in ______

Other Notes ______

Name ______________________ Nickname ______________

Age ________ Birthday ______________________ Death Date ______________

Gender ______________________ Species ______________________

Physical Appearance

Eye Color ______________________ Hair Color ______________________

Skin Color ______________________ Height ______________________

Build ______________________ ______________________

____

Role ______________________ Job/Career ______________________

Books this character appears in ______________________________

Other Notes ______________________________________

____

____

Name ______________________ Nickname ______________

Age ________ Birthday ______________________ Death Date ______________

Gender ______________________ Species ______________________

Physical Appearance

Eye Color ______________________ Hair Color ______________________

Skin Color ______________________ Height ______________________

Build ______________________ ______________________

____

Role ______________________ Job/Career ______________________

Books this character appears in ______________________________

Other Notes ______________________________________

____

____

Name ______________________ Nickname ______________

Age ______ Birthday ______________ Death Date ______________

Gender ______________ Species ______________

Physical Appearance

Eye Color ______________ Hair Color ______________

Skin Color ______________ Height ______________

Build ______________ ______________

____

Role ______________ Job/Career ______________

Books this character appears in ______________

Other Notes ______________________________

____

____

Name ______________________ Nickname ______________

Age ______ Birthday ______________ Death Date ______________

Gender ______________ Species ______________

Physical Appearance

Eye Color ______________ Hair Color ______________

Skin Color ______________ Height ______________

Build ______________ ______________

____

Role ______________ Job/Career ______________

Books this character appears in ______________

Other Notes ______________________________

____

____

Name ________________ Nickname ________________

Age ________ Birthday ________________ Death Date ________________

Gender ________________ Species ________________

Physical Appearance

Eye Color ________________ Hair Color ________________

Skin Color ________________ Height ________________

Build ________________ ________________

____

Role ________________ Job/Career ________________

Books this character appears in ________________

Other Notes ________________

____

____

Name ________________ Nickname ________________

Age ________ Birthday ________________ Death Date ________________

Gender ________________ Species ________________

Physical Appearance

Eye Color ________________ Hair Color ________________

Skin Color ________________ Height ________________

Build ________________ ________________

____

Role ________________ Job/Career ________________

Books this character appears in ________________

Other Notes ________________

____

____

Name ______________________ Nickname ______________

Age ________ Birthday ______________ Death Date ______________

Gender ______________ Species ______________

Physical Appearance

Eye Color ______________ Hair Color ______________

Skin Color ______________ Height ______________

Build ______________ ______________

____

Role ______________ Job/Career ______________

Books this character appears in ______________________

Other Notes ______________________________________

____

____

Name ______________________ Nickname ______________

Age ________ Birthday ______________ Death Date ______________

Gender ______________ Species ______________

Physical Appearance

Eye Color ______________ Hair Color ______________

Skin Color ______________ Height ______________

Build ______________ ______________

____

Role ______________ Job/Career ______________

Books this character appears in ______________________

Other Notes ______________________________________

____

____

Name ______________________ Nickname ______________

Age ________ Birthday ______________ Death Date ______________

Gender ______________ Species ______________

Physical Appearance

Eye Color ______________ Hair Color ______________

Skin Color ______________ Height ______________

Build ______________ ______________

Role ______________ Job/Career ______________

Books this character appears in ______________

Other Notes ______________

Name ______________________ Nickname ______________

Age ________ Birthday ______________ Death Date ______________

Gender ______________ Species ______________

Physical Appearance

Eye Color ______________ Hair Color ______________

Skin Color ______________ Height ______________

Build ______________ ______________

Role ______________ Job/Career ______________

Books this character appears in ______________

Other Notes ______________

Settings

Oooh… Settings! These are the places that your story happens. If our werewolf Luna lives at the Wolfieton Pack house, then you'd record the details of that setting here. Any location where a scene takes place should appear in this section.

If you've created a fictional world that requires a map, just pop to the end of the Settings section and you'll find four blank pages for all of your map-drawing needs.

"A rustic setting always suggests fantasy; to suggest science fiction, you need sheet metal and plastic. You need rivets."

Orson Scott Card

Location Name Wolfieton Pack house Residence, Business, or Other? Residence

Description Huge sprawling mansion deep in the mountains of Georgia. Driveway is gravel, long and winding from main asphalt road. Lawn is manicured in a circle around house for approx. 100 yards.

Books this setting appears in #1

Other Notes/Details Luna and higher-ranking wolves live in the packhouse. Jeannie (Caro's mom) is there a lot.

Location Name ______ Residence, Business, or Other? ______

Description ______

Books this setting appears in ______

Other Notes/Details ______

Location Name ______ Residence, Business, or Other? ______

Description ______

Books this setting appears in ______

Other Notes/Details ______

Location Name ______ Residence, Business, or Other? ______

Description ______

Books this setting appears in ______

Other Notes/Details ______

Location Name ______________ Residence, Business, or Other? ______

Description ______________

Books this setting appears in ______________

Other Notes/Details ______________

Location Name ______________ Residence, Business, or Other? ______

Description ______________

Books this setting appears in ______________

Other Notes/Details ______________

Location Name ______________ Residence, Business, or Other? ______

Description ______________

Books this setting appears in ______________

Other Notes/Details ______________

Location Name ______________________ Residence, Business, or Other? ____________

Description ____

____

____

Books this setting appears in ____

____

Other Notes/Details ____

____

____

Location Name ______________________ Residence, Business, or Other? ____________

Description ____

____

____

Books this setting appears in ____

____

Other Notes/Details ____

____

____

Location Name ______________________ Residence, Business, or Other? ____________

Description ____

____

____

Books this setting appears in ____

____

Other Notes/Details ____

____

____

Location Name ______________ Residence, Business, or Other? ______________

Description ______________

Books this setting appears in ______________

Other Notes/Details ______________

Location Name ______________ Residence, Business, or Other? ______________

Description ______________

Books this setting appears in ______________

Other Notes/Details ______________

Location Name ______________ Residence, Business, or Other? ______________

Description ______________

Books this setting appears in ______________

Other Notes/Details ______________

Location Name ______________________ Residence, Business, or Other? ____________

Description ____

Books this setting appears in ______________________________________

Other Notes/Details ______________________________________

Location Name ______________________ Residence, Business, or Other? ____________

Description ____

Books this setting appears in ______________________________________

Other Notes/Details ______________________________________

Location Name ______________________ Residence, Business, or Other? ____________

Description ____

Books this setting appears in ______________________________________

Other Notes/Details ______________________________________

Location Name ________________ Residence, Business, or Other? ________

Description ________________

Books this setting appears in ________________

Other Notes/Details ________________

Location Name ________________ Residence, Business, or Other? ________

Description ________________

Books this setting appears in ________________

Other Notes/Details ________________

Location Name ________________ Residence, Business, or Other? ________

Description ________________

Books this setting appears in ________________

Other Notes/Details ________________

Location Name ______________________ Residence, Business, or Other? ____________

Description ____

____

____

Books this setting appears in ____

____

Other Notes/Details ____

____

____

Location Name ______________________ Residence, Business, or Other? ____________

Description ____

____

____

Books this setting appears in ____

____

Other Notes/Details ____

____

____

Location Name ______________________ Residence, Business, or Other? ____________

Description ____

____

____

Books this setting appears in ____

____

Other Notes/Details ____

____

____

Location Name ______________ Residence, Business, or Other? ______

Description ______________

____

____

Books this setting appears in ______________

____

Other Notes/Details ______________

____

____

Location Name ______________ Residence, Business, or Other? ______

Description ______________

____

____

Books this setting appears in ______________

____

Other Notes/Details ______________

____

____

Location Name ______________ Residence, Business, or Other? ______

Description ______________

____

____

Books this setting appears in ______________

____

Other Notes/Details ______________

____

____

Location Name ______________________ Residence, Business, or Other? ____________

Description ____

____

____

Books this setting appears in ______________________________

____

Other Notes/Details ______________________________

____

____

Location Name ______________________ Residence, Business, or Other? ____________

Description ____

____

____

Books this setting appears in ______________________________

____

Other Notes/Details ______________________________

____

____

Location Name ______________________ Residence, Business, or Other? ____________

Description ____

____

____

Books this setting appears in ______________________________

____

Other Notes/Details ______________________________

____

____

Location Name ______________ Residence, Business, or Other? ______________

Description ______________

Books this setting appears in ______________

Other Notes/Details ______________

Location Name ______________ Residence, Business, or Other? ______________

Description ______________

Books this setting appears in ______________

Other Notes/Details ______________

Location Name ______________ Residence, Business, or Other? ______________

Description ______________

Books this setting appears in ______________

Other Notes/Details ______________

Location Name ____________ Residence, Business, or Other? ____________

Description ____________

Books this setting appears in ____________

Other Notes/Details ____________

Location Name ____________ Residence, Business, or Other? ____________

Description ____________

Books this setting appears in ____________

Other Notes/Details ____________

Location Name ____________ Residence, Business, or Other? ____________

Description ____________

Books this setting appears in ____________

Other Notes/Details ____________

Location Name ______________________ Residence, Business, or Other? __________

Description ____

____

____

Books this setting appears in ____

____

Other Notes/Details ____

____

____

Location Name ______________________ Residence, Business, or Other? __________

Description ____

____

____

Books this setting appears in ____

____

Other Notes/Details ____

____

____

Location Name ______________________ Residence, Business, or Other? __________

Description ____

____

____

Books this setting appears in ____

____

Other Notes/Details ____

____

____

Location Name ______________ Residence, Business, or Other? ______________

Description ______________

Books this setting appears in ______________

Other Notes/Details ______________

Location Name ______________ Residence, Business, or Other? ______________

Description ______________

Books this setting appears in ______________

Other Notes/Details ______________

Location Name ______________ Residence, Business, or Other? ______________

Description ______________

Books this setting appears in ______________

Other Notes/Details ______________

Location Name ____________ Residence, Business, or Other? ____________

Description ____________

Books this setting appears in ____________

Other Notes/Details ____________

Additional Notes

Map

Map

Map

Main Characters Caroline Wolfieton & Eric Hotterton

Chapter	Summary
1	Caroline is out for a night of fun and is hit on by Eric.
	POV Char Caroline Wolfieton Day/Time Day 1/Late Night
	Other Characters

Book # ______ *Title* ______

Main Characters ______

Chapter	Summary
1	POV Char ______ Day/Time ______ Other Characters ______
2	POV Char ______ Day/Time ______ Other Characters ______
3	POV Char ______ Day/Time ______ Other Characters ______
4	POV Char ______ Day/Time ______ Other Characters ______
5	POV Char ______ Day/Time ______ Other Characters ______
6	POV Char ______ Day/Time ______ Other Characters ______
7	POV Char ______ Day/Time ______ Other Characters ______

Chapter	Summary	
8		
	POV Char	Day/Time
	Other Characters	
9		
	POV Char	Day/Time
	Other Characters	
10		
	POV Char	Day/Time
	Other Characters	
11		
	POV Char	Day/Time
	Other Characters	
12		
	POV Char	Day/Time
	Other Characters	
13		
	POV Char	Day/Time
	Other Characters	
14		
	POV Char	Day/Time
	Other Characters	

Chapter	Summary	
15		
	POV Char	Day/Time
	Other Characters	
16		
	POV Char	Day/Time
	Other Characters	
17		
	POV Char	Day/Time
	Other Characters	
18		
	POV Char	Day/Time
	Other Characters	
19		
	POV Char	Day/Time
	Other Characters	
20		
	POV Char	Day/Time
	Other Characters	
21		
	POV Char	Day/Time
	Other Characters	

Chapter	Summary	
22		
	POV Char	Day/Time
	Other Characters	
23		
	POV Char	Day/Time
	Other Characters	
24		
	POV Char	Day/Time
	Other Characters	
25		
	POV Char	Day/Time
	Other Characters	
26		
	POV Char	Day/Time
	Other Characters	
27		
	POV Char	Day/Time
	Other Characters	
28		
	POV Char	Day/Time
	Other Characters	

Chapter	Summary	
29		
	POV Char	Day/Time
	Other Characters	
30		
	POV Char	Day/Time
	Other Characters	
31		
	POV Char	Day/Time
	Other Characters	
32		
	POV Char	Day/Time
	Other Characters	
33		
	POV Char	Day/Time
	Other Characters	
34		
	POV Char	Day/Time
	Other Characters	
35		
	POV Char	Day/Time
	Other Characters	

Additional Notes

Book # ______ *Title* ______

Main Characters ______

Chapter	Summary	
1		
	POV Char	Day/Time
	Other Characters	
2		
	POV Char	Day/Time
	Other Characters	
3		
	POV Char	Day/Time
	Other Characters	
4		
	POV Char	Day/Time
	Other Characters	
5		
	POV Char	Day/Time
	Other Characters	
6		
	POV Char	Day/Time
	Other Characters	
7		
	POV Char	Day/Time
	Other Characters	

Chapter	Summary	
8	POV Char	Day/Time
	Other Characters	
9	POV Char	Day/Time
	Other Characters	
10	POV Char	Day/Time
	Other Characters	
11	POV Char	Day/Time
	Other Characters	
12	POV Char	Day/Time
	Other Characters	
13	POV Char	Day/Time
	Other Characters	
14	POV Char	Day/Time
	Other Characters	

Chapter	Summary	
15		
	POV Char	Day/Time
	Other Characters	
16		
	POV Char	Day/Time
	Other Characters	
17		
	POV Char	Day/Time
	Other Characters	
18		
	POV Char	Day/Time
	Other Characters	
19		
	POV Char	Day/Time
	Other Characters	
20		
	POV Char	Day/Time
	Other Characters	
21		
	POV Char	Day/Time
	Other Characters	

Chapter	Summary	
22		
	POV Char	Day/Time
	Other Characters	
23		
	POV Char	Day/Time
	Other Characters	
24		
	POV Char	Day/Time
	Other Characters	
25		
	POV Char	Day/Time
	Other Characters	
26		
	POV Char	Day/Time
	Other Characters	
27		
	POV Char	Day/Time
	Other Characters	
28		
	POV Char	Day/Time
	Other Characters	

Chapter	Summary	
29		
	POV Char	Day/Time
	Other Characters	
30		
	POV Char	Day/Time
	Other Characters	
31		
	POV Char	Day/Time
	Other Characters	
32		
	POV Char	Day/Time
	Other Characters	
33		
	POV Char	Day/Time
	Other Characters	
34		
	POV Char	Day/Time
	Other Characters	
35		
	POV Char	Day/Time
	Other Characters	

Additional Notes

Book # ______ *Title* ______

Main Characters ______

Chapter	Summary	
1		
	POV Char	Day/Time
	Other Characters	
2		
	POV Char	Day/Time
	Other Characters	
3		
	POV Char	Day/Time
	Other Characters	
4		
	POV Char	Day/Time
	Other Characters	
5		
	POV Char	Day/Time
	Other Characters	
6		
	POV Char	Day/Time
	Other Characters	
7		
	POV Char	Day/Time
	Other Characters	

Chapter	Summary	
8		
	POV Char	Day/Time
	Other Characters	
9		
	POV Char	Day/Time
	Other Characters	
10		
	POV Char	Day/Time
	Other Characters	
11		
	POV Char	Day/Time
	Other Characters	
12		
	POV Char	Day/Time
	Other Characters	
13		
	POV Char	Day/Time
	Other Characters	
14		
	POV Char	Day/Time
	Other Characters	

Chapter	Summary	
15		
	POV Char	Day/Time
	Other Characters	
16		
	POV Char	Day/Time
	Other Characters	
17		
	POV Char	Day/Time
	Other Characters	
18		
	POV Char	Day/Time
	Other Characters	
19		
	POV Char	Day/Time
	Other Characters	
20		
	POV Char	Day/Time
	Other Characters	
21		
	POV Char	Day/Time
	Other Characters	

Chapter	Summary	
22		
	POV Char	Day/Time
	Other Characters	
23		
	POV Char	Day/Time
	Other Characters	
24		
	POV Char	Day/Time
	Other Characters	
25		
	POV Char	Day/Time
	Other Characters	
26		
	POV Char	Day/Time
	Other Characters	
27		
	POV Char	Day/Time
	Other Characters	
28		
	POV Char	Day/Time
	Other Characters	

Chapter	Summary	
29		
	POV Char	Day/Time
	Other Characters	
30		
	POV Char	Day/Time
	Other Characters	
31		
	POV Char	Day/Time
	Other Characters	
32		
	POV Char	Day/Time
	Other Characters	
33		
	POV Char	Day/Time
	Other Characters	
34		
	POV Char	Day/Time
	Other Characters	
35		
	POV Char	Day/Time
	Other Characters	

Additional Notes

Book # ______ *Title* ______

Main Characters ______

Chapter	Summary
1	
	POV Char Day/Time
	Other Characters
2	
	POV Char Day/Time
	Other Characters
3	
	POV Char Day/Time
	Other Characters
4	
	POV Char Day/Time
	Other Characters
5	
	POV Char Day/Time
	Other Characters
6	
	POV Char Day/Time
	Other Characters
7	
	POV Char Day/Time
	Other Characters

Chapter	Summary	
8		
	POV Char	Day/Time
	Other Characters	
9		
	POV Char	Day/Time
	Other Characters	
10		
	POV Char	Day/Time
	Other Characters	
11		
	POV Char	Day/Time
	Other Characters	
12		
	POV Char	Day/Time
	Other Characters	
13		
	POV Char	Day/Time
	Other Characters	
14		
	POV Char	Day/Time
	Other Characters	

Chapter	Summary	
15		
	POV Char	Day/Time
	Other Characters	
16		
	POV Char	Day/Time
	Other Characters	
17		
	POV Char	Day/Time
	Other Characters	
18		
	POV Char	Day/Time
	Other Characters	
19		
	POV Char	Day/Time
	Other Characters	
20		
	POV Char	Day/Time
	Other Characters	
21		
	POV Char	Day/Time
	Other Characters	

Chapter	Summary	
22		
	POV Char	Day/Time
	Other Characters	
23		
	POV Char	Day/Time
	Other Characters	
24		
	POV Char	Day/Time
	Other Characters	
25		
	POV Char	Day/Time
	Other Characters	
26		
	POV Char	Day/Time
	Other Characters	
27		
	POV Char	Day/Time
	Other Characters	
28		
	POV Char	Day/Time
	Other Characters	

Chapter	Summary	
29		
	POV Char	Day/Time
	Other Characters	
30		
	POV Char	Day/Time
	Other Characters	
31		
	POV Char	Day/Time
	Other Characters	
32		
	POV Char	Day/Time
	Other Characters	
33		
	POV Char	Day/Time
	Other Characters	
34		
	POV Char	Day/Time
	Other Characters	
35		
	POV Char	Day/Time
	Other Characters	

Additional Notes

Book # ______ *Title* ______

Main Characters ______

Chapter	Summary	
1		
	POV Char	Day/Time
	Other Characters	
2		
	POV Char	Day/Time
	Other Characters	
3		
	POV Char	Day/Time
	Other Characters	
4		
	POV Char	Day/Time
	Other Characters	
5		
	POV Char	Day/Time
	Other Characters	
6		
	POV Char	Day/Time
	Other Characters	
7		
	POV Char	Day/Time
	Other Characters	

Chapter	Summary	
8		
	POV Char	Day/Time
	Other Characters	
9		
	POV Char	Day/Time
	Other Characters	
10		
	POV Char	Day/Time
	Other Characters	
11		
	POV Char	Day/Time
	Other Characters	
12		
	POV Char	Day/Time
	Other Characters	
13		
	POV Char	Day/Time
	Other Characters	
14		
	POV Char	Day/Time
	Other Characters	

Chapter	Summary	
15		
	POV Char	Day/Time
	Other Characters	
16		
	POV Char	Day/Time
	Other Characters	
17		
	POV Char	Day/Time
	Other Characters	
18		
	POV Char	Day/Time
	Other Characters	
19		
	POV Char	Day/Time
	Other Characters	
20		
	POV Char	Day/Time
	Other Characters	
21		
	POV Char	Day/Time
	Other Characters	

Chapter	Summary	
22		
	POV Char	Day/Time
	Other Characters	
23		
	POV Char	Day/Time
	Other Characters	
24		
	POV Char	Day/Time
	Other Characters	
25		
	POV Char	Day/Time
	Other Characters	
26		
	POV Char	Day/Time
	Other Characters	
27		
	POV Char	Day/Time
	Other Characters	
28		
	POV Char	Day/Time
	Other Characters	

Chapter	Summary	
29		
	POV Char	Day/Time
	Other Characters	
30		
	POV Char	Day/Time
	Other Characters	
31		
	POV Char	Day/Time
	Other Characters	
32		
	POV Char	Day/Time
	Other Characters	
33		
	POV Char	Day/Time
	Other Characters	
34		
	POV Char	Day/Time
	Other Characters	
35		
	POV Char	Day/Time
	Other Characters	

Additional Notes

Notes

You've reached the end of the workbook! *high five* This section is for any other notes you might have about the series that doesn't fit anywhere else. Got a title idea? Make a note! Think of an awesome idea for the next book in the series? Jot that solid gold down right away!

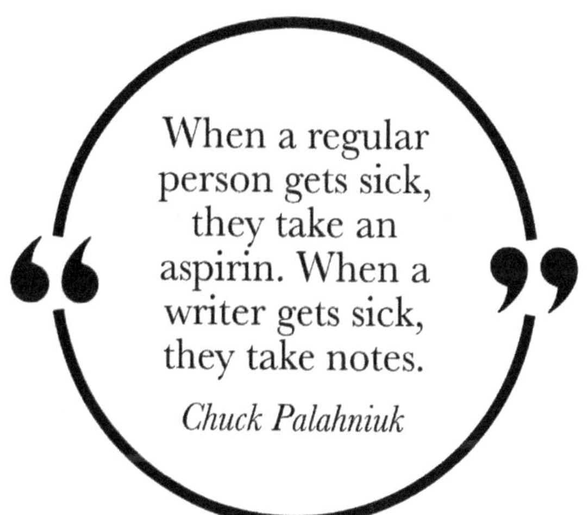

About the Author

Celia Kyle is a New York Times and USA Today bestselling author of paranormal and science fiction romance, as well as non-fiction for authors. She is also the creator of the bestselling Howls Romance and In the Stars Romance lines.

As a longstanding veteran in the publishing industry, Celia has spent over a decade struggling to keep track of series details. With over eighty books spread across eighteen series, organization isn't an option--it's a necessity. She created 'The Writer's Complete Series Bible Workbook' to finally gather those important details in one place.

Today she lives in central Florida and writes full-time with the support of her loving husband and two finicky cats.

Website – www.celiakyle.com
Facebook – www.facebook.com/authorceliakyle

Other author-focused print books, digital workbooks, and printable PDFs can be found on the Novel Notes website at www.novelnotesbooks.com Be sure to stop by and download your FREE copy of *The Writer's Visual Timeline.*

www.ingramcontent.com/pod-product-compliance
Lightning Source LLC
Chambersburg PA
CBHW080557030426
42336CB00019B/3232
* 9 7 8 1 6 8 0 3 9 0 0 2 5 *